Mr Monty

By Melinda Lem
Art by Romulo Reyes III

Library For All Ltd.

Library For All is an Australian not for profit organisation with a mission to make knowledge accessible to all via an innovative digital library solution. Visit us at libraryforall.org

Mr Monty

First published 2018
This edition published 2021

Published by Library For All Ltd
Email: info@libraryforall.org
URL: libraryforall.org

This book was previously produced by the Together For Education Partnership supported by the Australian Government through the Papua New Guinea-Australia Partnership.

This edition was made possible by the generous support of the Education Cooperation Program.

Original illustrations by Romulo Reyes III

Mr Monty
Lem, Melinda
ISBN: 978-1-922621-23-8
SKU01611

Mr Monty

Hello Mr Monty! It's me, Veisi.

I hope you remember me. How are you?

I just had my lunch, and I brought some for you!

Here is a banana. There you go boy. Eat up.

So, now can we go for a ride?
Hold on steady.
I will count.
One, two, three and here I go.

Gallop, gallop, gallop.
Past the green trees.
Faster Mr Monty! Let's
try to reach the top of
the hill.

Gallop, gallop, gallop.
Up the hill we go!
Steady Mr Monty! I hope
I am not too heavy.

Gallop, gallop, gallop.
Wow! Look at the view!
I never knew Visale was
so beautiful.

Oh Mr Monty, I wish I was on holiday, but it's time to go home for my afternoon classes.

Gallop, gallop, gallop.
Down the hill we go.

Gallop, gallop, gallop.
Round and round the
trees.

Gallop, gallop, gallop.
Watch out for the
puddles!

Gallop, gallop, gallop.
Thank you for the ride
Mr Monty.

You can use these questions to talk about this book with your family, friends and teachers.

What did you learn from this book?

Describe this book in one word. Funny? Scary? Colourful? Interesting?

How did this book make you feel when you finished reading it?

What was your favourite part of this book?

About the contributors

Library For All works with authors and illustrators from around the world to develop diverse, relevant, high quality stories for young readers. Visit libraryforall.org for the latest news on writers' workshop events, submission guidelines and other creative opportunities.

Did you enjoy this book?

We have hundreds more expertly curated original stories to choose from.

We work in partnership with authors, educators, cultural advisors, governments and NGOs to bring the joy of reading to children everywhere.

Did you know?

We create global impact in these fields by embracing the United Nations Sustainable Development Goals.

www.ingramcontent.com/pod-product-compliance
Lightning Source LLC
Chambersburg PA
CBHW041534070426
42452CB00045B/2873